Mark H. Hoeksema

Studies in
ROMANS

REFORMED
FREE PUBLISHING
ASSOCIATION

Jenison, Michigan

Scripture cited is taken from the Authorized (King James) Version

Reformed Free Publishing Association
1894 Georgetown Center Drive
Jenison MI 49428
616-457-5970
www.rfpa.org
mail@rfpa.org

Book design and typesetting by Erika Kiel

ISBN 978-1-936054-92-3
LCCN 2015952420

Acknowledgement

I am indebted to Rev. Rodney Kleyn for the use of some of his unpublished study material on the book of Romans.

Suggested Study Resources

Primary

Herman Hoeksema, *Righteous by Faith Alone* (Reformed Free Publishing Association)

William Hendriksen, *New Testament Commentary: Romans* (Baker Book House)

John Calvin, *Commentary on the Epistle of Paul the Apostle to the Romans*

Stuart Olyott, *The Gospel as It Really Is: Romans* (Evangelical Press)

David Steel and Curtis Thomas, *Romans: An Interpretive Outline* (Presbyterian and Reformed Publishing Company)

Secondary

Martin Luther, *Commentary on the Epistle to the Romans* (Kregel Publications)

R. C. Sproul, *The Righteous Shall Live by Faith* (Crossway Books)

F. F. Bruce, *Tyndale New Testament Commentaries (Romans)* (Inter-Varsity Press)

John Murray and F. F. Bruce, *The Epistle to the Romans* (Wm. B. Eerdmans Publishing Company)

Charles Hodge, *A Commentary on the Epistle to the Romans* (Banner of Truth)

William G. T. Shedd, *A Critical and Doctrinal Commentary on the Epistle of Paul to the Romans* (Klock and Klock)

Some of these books can be obtained either online or from a used book store. A good Bible dictionary or encyclopedia will also be helpful.

Introduction

The Importance of Romans

No other book of the Bible so completely and systematically defines and explains the doctrines of the Christian faith and their application to living the Christian life as does Romans. Paul mentions and explains in varying degrees the truths of the faith: sin, law, judgment, faith, works, grace, justification, sanctification, hope, the church, the place of Jews and Gentiles in God's purpose, sovereign double predestination, the meaning of the Old Testament, citizenship in a wicked world, and the principles of piety and ethics (Steele and Thomas, *An Interpretive Outline*).

The Writer of Romans

The author of Romans is the Holy Spirit; Romans is divinely inspired and belongs to the canon of scripture. The writer is the apostle Paul. Paul was born in Tarsus of Cilicia and was a Roman citizen. He was educated in the Jewish tradition in the strict sect of the Pharisees, and he studied under the noted rabbi Gamaliel; he was a Hebrew of the Hebrews. In the earliest days of the church he was a leader in persecuting the Christians until his conversion on the Damascus road. He was called by Christ to be an apostle to the Gentiles. He went on three missionary journeys, preaching the gospel of Christ and establishing churches in many locations. Subsequently he wrote letters to many of these churches, which are preserved for us in the New Testament. Later in life he was sent to Rome to stand trial before Caesar. He was imprisoned there for a time, released for a time, and then imprisoned once again before being killed at Rome.

The Occasion for Romans

Paul wrote the letter to the Romans from Corinth while on his third missionary journey. The likely date of this writing was AD 57 or 58. Paul wanted to visit the church at Rome, but was unable to do so. The letter was probably written to prepare the way for a future possible visit. There were apparently no significant problems in the Roman church. Paul's letter is therefore instructional and preventive, not corrective. He writes to the Romans as Christian friends, even though most of them he does not know personally.

The Church in Rome

Scripture does not tell us much about the church at Rome. We do not know exactly how the Roman church came into existence. Certain it is that Peter was not the founder of the church, as the Roman Catholics allege in order to promote their contention that Peter was the first pope. We know that Peter was there later, but not at this time. The most likely explanation for the origin of the church at Rome is that it was founded by Jews of the dispersion and proselytes (converts) to the faith who had made their homes in Rome. We read in Acts 2:10 that visitors from Rome, both Jews and proselytes, were among those present at Pentecost, and were numbered among the believers. The obvious conclusion is that when they returned to Rome, they brought the gospel of Christ with them; no doubt they proclaimed that gospel to the Gentile Romans among whom they lived, and the church came into being.

We do not know the size of the church at Rome. We do know the names of some of the members (ch. 16), although we know little or nothing about most of them. We do know from the language and topics dealt with in the epistle that the Roman church was a mix of Jews and Gentiles.

The Purpose of Romans

It is difficult to specify a single purpose that Paul expresses in the book. Rather, there are several related purposes to which we can point. Although he had never been to Rome, Paul was concerned with the welfare of the church there.

His purpose was to set forth in a clear and logical manner the Christian doctrines and in this way to forestall any false teachings that might arise. There are hints in his epistle that point to possible problems looming on the horizon, specifically the opposition of Judaizers and the error of antinomianism. Thus the apostle wants the church to be knowledgeable and well-grounded in the faith of Christ.

His purpose was also to strengthen the church in its hope. The word *hope* is used far more frequently in Romans than in any other book of the Bible, indicating that hope is a very important aspect of the Christian life.

His purpose was to instruct the mixed Jew and Gentile church concerning the rejection of the Jews as a nation and the inclusion of the Gentiles in the church.

His purpose was to exhort and admonish the church concerning the Christian life, something that is always necessary for the church.

Theme and Division of Romans

There is no single theme in the epistle from which the apostle deviates. Yet we can say that the main idea of Romans is justification by grace through faith (Rom. 3:24, 3:28, 5:1).

The book is best divided into three parts:
1. Justification by faith and its implications (chapters 1–8).
2. The rejection of the Jews and the inclusion of the Gentiles (chapters 9–11).
3. Practical exhortations and personal matters (chapters 12–16).

Methodology

The question format of this study guide is intended to help God's people define and understand Paul's concepts and terms, as well as their relationships to one another. As much as possible the questions are intentionally leading, with the goal of fostering discussion and assisting in the understanding of Romans, whether in Bible study societies or on a personal level. To the extent that the questions are accurately answered, the student of Romans will gain an understanding of the epistle.

Mark H. Hoeksema

Romans 1

Romans 1:1–7

Paul introduces himself and greets the church of Rome.

1. Paul calls himself a servant (literally, "slave") of Christ (v. 1). What does this term imply?

2. He also calls himself an apostle (v. 1). What was an apostle?

3. Why does Paul refer to the Old Testament in verses 2–3?

4. What does it mean that Christ is declared (appointed) to be the Son in power and according to the Spirit of holiness (v. 4)?

5. What does the resurrection of Christ prove (v. 4)?

6. Who are the "we" who have received grace and apostleship (v. 5)?

7. How is "for obedience to the faith among all nations" related to receiving grace and apostleship (v. 5)?

8. In what two ways does Paul describe the church of Rome? What do these terms mean (v. 7)?

9. What do "grace" and "peace" mean?

Romans 1:8–14

Paul expresses his desire to visit the church at Rome.

1. Why is Paul thankful for "all" the saints (v. 8)?

2. Why is he thankful to God (v. 8)?

3. How often does he pray for the saints (v. 9)? What do we learn from this?

4. What is intercessory prayer? Why is such prayer necessary?

5. For what is Paul thankful (v. 8)?

6. What is Paul's primary desire (v. 10)?

7. What three reasons does Paul give for wanting to visit the Roman church (vv. 11–13)?

8. What is the comfort of "mutual faith" (v. 12)?

9. Who are the Greeks and the barbarians (v. 14)?

10. What does it mean that he is a debtor to both?

Romans 1:15–17

Paul defines the gospel.

1. Why is Paul so eager to preach the gospel to the Roman church (vv. 14–15)?

2. What is the gospel of Christ—the Bible, the preaching, the message (v. 15)?

3. How is the gospel the power unto salvation (v. 16)?

4. Is the gospel an offer or a command? Compare the Arminian and Calvinistic views.

5. Is faith a condition to salvation (v. 16)?

6. What is the content of the gospel (v. 17)?

7. What is the "righteousness of God" (v. 17)?

8. What does it mean that righteousness is revealed "from faith to faith?"

9. What is the relation between faith and being just (v. 17)?

10. Why does the gospel come to the Jew first and then to the Greek (v. 16)?

11. What is the twofold effect of the gospel?

12. Why might one be ashamed of the gospel?

13. How do these verses encourage us not to be ashamed of the gospel?

Romans 1:18–32

Paul describes the wrath of God against the natural man. This passage shows the necessity of justification.

1. About whom is Paul writing—Jews, Gentiles, or unregenerate man in general (v. 18)?

2. What is the relation between this passage and the preceding ("For," v. 18)?

3. What is the wrath of God?

4. Against what is it revealed (v. 18)?

5. Can men know that God's wrath is revealed against them? How (v. 19)?

6. What does holding the truth in unrighteousness mean (v. 18)?

7. How is verse 19 a reason ("Because") for the revelation of God's wrath (v. 18)?

8. What two things can men know about God apart from the gospel (v. 20)?

9. How do they know these (v. 20)?

10. Is this knowledge sufficient to condemn them (v. 20)? Apart from the gospel, how is this possible?

11. Is their knowledge sufficient for them to be saved?

12. What do men do with their knowledge (v. 21)?

13. What is the connection between verse 21 and being wise and being fools (v. 22)?

14. Instead of serving God, what do they do (vv. 23, 25)?

15. What is God's reaction to this (v. 24, vv. 26–28)?

16. What does it mean that God "gave them up" (v. 24) to their immorality?

17. To what sin do verses 26–27 refer?

18. Is it correct to say that this is the ultimate manifestation of sin?

19. Why does scripture severely condemn homosexuality?

20. What should be our attitude toward the homosexual and his sin?

21. The twenty-two terms in verses 29–31 can be divided as follows:
    The first five describe categories of sins.
    The next five describe specific sins.
    The last twelve describe those who commit these sins.

22. What does each of the above terms mean?

23. How does verse 32 show the deliberate nature of sin?

24. How can we be guilty of taking pleasure in the sins of others (v. 32)?

Romans 2

Romans 2:1–16

Paul speaks of God's judgment on the sinners described in chapter 1:18–32.

1. How does "Therefore" connect chapter 1 and chapter 2?

2. What is the difference in viewpoint between chapter 1 and chapter 2?

3. To whom does Paul write (vv. 1, 3)?

4. Who is the "we" of verse 2?

5. What is the biblical idea of judging (vv. 1–3)?

6. Is it right or wrong to pass judgment on others? Why or why not?

7. What point does Paul make in verses 1–3 (see Matt. 7:1–4)?

8. What attitude does Paul address in verses 4–5?

9. What are the goodness, forbearance, and long-suffering of God (v. 4)?

10. What is it to despise these virtues of God (v. 4)?

11. What does it mean that the goodness of God leads to repentance (v. 4)? Is this always true?

12. What are the day of wrath and the revelation of God's righteous judgment (v. 5)?

13. What does it mean that God will judge every man "according to his deeds" (v. 6)?

    If you have faith, your deeds should show it

14. What does it mean to treasure up wrath (v. 5)?

15. What is God's positive judgment (vv. 7, 10) according to the principle of verse 6?

16. What is God's negative judgment (vv. 8–9)?

17. Why do both judgments come upon the Jews first and then the Gentiles (vv. 9–10)?

18. What is "respect of persons" (v. 11)?

19. Why is there no respect of persons with God?

20. What does it mean to sin and to "perish without law" (v. 12)? Of whom is this true?

Non Jews Gentiles

21. What does it mean to sin in the law and to be judged by the law (v. 12)? Of whom is this true?

22. How is the judgment of those in the law different from those without the law (v. 12)?

23. Why are not the hearers but the doers of the law justified (v. 13)?

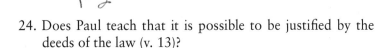

Romans 21:3

24. Does Paul teach that it is possible to be justified by the deeds of the law (v. 13)?

No

25. What are the things contained in the law (v. 14)?

26. How are the Gentiles a law unto themselves?

27. What is the work of the law in distinction from the law itself (v. 15)?

28. How is this work written in their hearts (v. 15)?

29. What is man's conscience (v. 15)?

30. How do the Gentiles either accuse or excuse themselves (v. 15)?

31. How can the Gentiles be condemned if they are without the law (vv. 14–15)?

32. All of this happens in the day of judgment. How does this happen according to Paul's gospel (v. 16)?

Prayers:
- *Porter's neighbor Chris Doody*
- *Marcia Boet*
- *Kay Espinosa - back surgery*
- *Diane*
- *Aunt Joann*
- *Ken*

Romans 2:17–29

Paul describes Jewish self-exaltation and hypocrisy.

1. What does it mean that the Jews rested in the law and made their boast in God (v. 17)?

   Privilege .

2. Verses 18–20 describe characteristics of the Jews:

   a. They know God's will and approve the more excellent things. What do these clauses mean?

      given the law

   b. They are confident that they are guides of the blind and a light to those in darkness. Who are the blind and those in darkness?

      They are "full" of themselves

   c. They are instructors of the foolish and teachers of babes. Who are the foolish and the babes?

3. What is the form of knowledge and of truth in the law (v. 20)?

4. What is the point of Paul's questions in verses 21–23?

5. What is the consequence of hypocrisy for the church (v. 24)?

False teachings among gentiles

6. How does circumcision profit if the law is kept (v. 25)? Is this possible?

7. How can circumcision become uncircumcision (v. 25)?

8. Of whom could Paul be thinking in verses 25–26? For what were they known?

   non-circumcised

9. What is uncircumcision which is by nature (v. 27)? How can it judge?

10. What contrast does Paul draw in verses 28–29? Who is a true Jew and what is true circumcision?

11. How does this contrast apply to us?

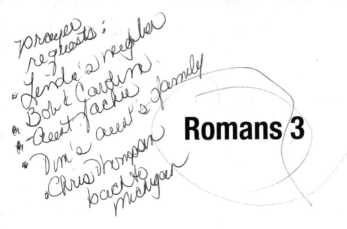

Romans 3

Romans 3:1–8

Paul answers three objections against God's righteousness.

1. What is the objection of verse 1?

   Is there a "place" for circumcision too? still?

2. What is Paul's answer in verse 2?

   Yes - they are still "chosen"

3. What are the oracles of God?

4. What is the objection raised in verse 3?

   What is fate of those unable to keep law?

5. What is Paul's answer in verse 4?

   Only God is righteous

6. How does the quotation from Psalm 51:4 prove Paul's point?

   My sinning separates me from God and only God is capable of restoration

7. What objection is raised in verse 5?

8. How does Paul answer this objection?

9. Who are those who raise this objection (v. 8)?

10. Why is their condemnation just?

Romans 3:9–18

Paul proves universal depravity to demonstrate the necessity of justification.

1. To what conclusion ("What then?") does Paul lead in verse 9?

    Jews

2. Who are the "we" in verse 9?

    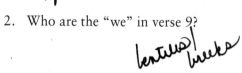

3. When Paul asks (v. 9), "Are we better than they," of whom is he speaking?

4. How has Paul previously proved that both Jews and Gentiles are under sin (v. 9)?

5. What scripture passages does Paul quote in verses 10–18?

6. Why does Paul quote from the Old Testament?

7. Who are described in verses 10–18?

8. What point does Paul make in verses 10–12?

9. Why does Paul single out sins of the tongue (vv. 13–14)?

10. To what expressions of man's sinfulness do verses 15–17 refer?

11. What is the basic reason for man's sinfulness and depravity (v. 18)?

Romans 3:19–31

Paul describes the righteousness of God in contrast to man's wickedness.

1. To what does "the law" refer (v. 19)?

OT · 10 comm, mosaic, law

2. Who are those who are under the law (v. 19)?

3. What is the purpose of the law (v. 19)?

4. What conclusion ("Therefore") does Paul draw from man's depravity (v. 20)?

5. What are the deeds of the law (v. 20)?

6. Why cannot anyone be justified by the deeds of the law (v. 20)?

7. In contrast, the righteousness of God is manifested. What does it mean that this righteousness is without the law (v. 21)?

8. Does God ignore the law in this righteousness?

9. What is the only way to be righteous before God (v. 22)?

10. What does "there is no difference" (v. 22) mean?

11. Why is there no difference (v. 23)?

12. What is the meaning of justification (v. 24)?

13. What does it mean to be justified "freely by grace" (v. 24)?

14. What is the meaning of "redemption" (v. 24)?

15. What words in verse 25 point to the truth of sovereign predestination?

16. What is a propitiation (v. 25)?

17. What are "sins that are past" (v. 25)?

18. What is the forbearance of God? How is it related to the remission of sins (v. 25)?

19. How is God the justifier of those who believe (v. 26)?

20. What is the boasting of which Paul speaks (v. 27)?

21. Why is boasting excluded (v. 27)?

22. What is the law of faith (v. 27)?

23. What is Paul's conclusion (vv. 28–29)?

24. What does it mean that God justifies the circumcision *by* faith and uncircumcision *through* faith (v. 30)?

25. To whom do these groups refer?

26. How do we establish the law rather than making it void (v. 31)?

Prayer Requests:

Hymn Quiz

Romans 4

Paul uses Abraham as an example of the truth that righteousness is not by the works of the law, but by faith. Abraham is the father not of those who have the law, but of those who believe.

1. Why does Paul use Abraham as proof that salvation is by faith and not by works (vv. 3–5)?

2. Did Abraham have reason to glory before God (v. 2)?

3. Who is "him that worketh?" What does it mean that his reward is reckoned of debt?

4. What was counted to Abraham for righteousness (v. 5)? Was his righteousness meritorious?

5. How is the faith of one who believes in Christ counted for righteousness (v. 5)?

6. What does it mean that God imputes righteousness (v. 6)?

7. How does Psalm 32:1–2 teach justification by faith (vv. 7–8)?

8. How did David learn this truth personally?

9. Is there a difference between forgiveness (v. 7) and righteousness (v. 6)?

10. In light of possible influence by Judaizers, what new thought does Paul introduce in verse 9?

11. How does Paul prove from Abraham's history that circumcision is not essential to salvation (vv. 11–12)?

12. If faith was reckoned as righteousness (v. 9) while Abraham was in uncircumcision (v. 10), why was circumcision necessary?

13. What is a seal (v. 11)?

14. How was circumcision a seal of the righteousness of faith (v. 11)?

15. Is circumcision necessary for salvation (see 1 Cor. 7:19, Gal. 6:15)?

16. How was Abraham the father of the circumcision (v. 11) and the father of the uncircumcision (v. 12)?

17. How was the promise to Abraham fulfilled (v. 13)?

18. How is faith made void and the promise of no effect (v. 14)?

19. How does the law work wrath (v. 15)?

20. Who are Abraham's children (vv. 16–17)?

21. Why is God described (v. 17) in terms of the resurrection and the work of creation?

22. How is Abraham's faith described in verses 17–21?

23. For whose sake is the truth of the imputation of faith written (vv. 23–24)?

24. What does verse 25 teach about the death of Christ?

25. What does verse 25 teach about the resurrection of Christ?

Romans 5

Romans 5:1–11

Paul makes a transition from the manner of justification to the fruits of justification.

1. What is the first benefit of justification (v. 1)?

2. What is the foundation of this peace?

3. Is peace objective or subjective?

4. What benefits are mentioned in verse 2?

5. What does access mean (v. 2)? To what do we have access?

6. What are tribulations (v. 3)?

7. What does it mean to glory in them? How can we and why do we?

8. How does tribulation work patience (v. 3)? What is patience?

9. How does patience work experience (v. 4)? What is experience?

10. How does experience work hope (v. 4)? What is hope?

11. What does it mean that hope does not make ashamed (v. 5)?

12. Does verse 5 refer to God's loving us or our loving God?

13. Who are the ungodly in verse 6?

14. Does verse 6 imply a supralapsarian or an infralapsarian view of the order of salvation?

15. What example does Paul use to demonstrate the greatness of God's love (v. 7)?

16. What is substitutionary atonement as taught in verses 6–8?

17. What does "commendeth" mean (v. 8)?

18. What does "much more" mean (v. 9)? Much more than what?

19. What does "much more" (v. 10) mean? What is the comparison drawn?

20. What is the consequence of being justified by Christ's blood (v. 9)?

21. In what do we rejoice (v. 11)?

Romans 5:12–21

Paul teaches the headship of Adam and of Christ.

1. How do verses 12, 15, 17–19 teach the headship of Adam?

2. When Adam sinned, who also sinned (v. 12)?

3. How is this possible? Is this fair?

4. What is the consequence of this sin?

5. What is corporate responsibility? Can you give examples from scripture and from life?

6. What is a legal head or representative?

7. What does it mean that sin is not imputed in the absence of law (v. 13)?

8. If this is true, how could death reign from Adam to Moses (v. 14)?

9. What does it mean that Adam was the figure of him who was to come (v. 14)?

10. How are the offence and the free gift different (v. 15)?

11. Who are the "many" mentioned twice in verse 15?

12. What is the contrast between the judgment of one to condemnation and the free gift of many offences unto justification (v. 16)?

13. What is the contrast drawn in verse 17?

14. What does it mean to reign in life by Jesus Christ (v. 17)?

15. When verse 18 says that as judgment came upon all men to condemnation, so the free gift came upon all men to justification, does this teach a universal atonement?

16. Who are the "many" mentioned twice in verse 19?

17. What is the relation between the law and grace (vv. 20–21)?

Romans 6

Paul teaches that holiness is a second fruit of justification.

1. What objection is raised against Paul's teaching of justification by grace alone (v. 1)?

2. Is this question a theoretical conclusion or a practical consequence?

3. Does verse 2 teach that we are sinless?

4. What does it mean to be dead to sin (v. 2)?

5. What is it to be baptized into Christ and into his death (v. 3)?

6. What is the purpose of our being buried with Christ (v. 4)?

7. What does baptism have to do with burial and death (v. 4)?

8. What is walking in newness of life (v. 4)?

9. What analogy does Paul use in verse 5? What other scripture uses this analogy?

10. Do verses 5–10 refer to a spiritual or a bodily resurrection?

11. What is our old man (v. 6)?

12. What is the destruction of the body of sin (v. 6)?

13. In what way are we dead? How are we freed from sin (v. 7)?

14. What does it mean to be dead with Christ and also to live with him (v. 8)?

15. Why does death have no more dominion over Christ (vv. 9–10)?

16. According to verse 11, what conclusion should be drawn from verses 9–10?

17. What are our members (v. 13)?

18. What does it mean not to yield them as instruments of unrighteousness unto sin (v. 13)?

19. What does it mean that we are not under the law but under grace (v. 14)?

20. Is this a license to sin (v. 15)? Who teach this error?

21. What principle does Paul state in verse 16?

22. What does it mean to obey from the heart the form of doctrine delivered to us (v. 17)?

23. What contrast does Paul draw in verses 18–20?

24. What does it mean that Paul speaks after the manner of men because of the infirmity of our flesh (v. 19)?

25. What is "to iniquity unto iniquity" (v. 19)?

26. What practical argument does Paul make for holiness in verses 21–23?

27. What are the wages of sin (v. 23)?

Romans 7

Paul speaks of the Christian's relation to the law.

1. To whom does Paul speak in verse 1?

2. Of what law does he speak in verse 1 and in many other verses in this chapter?

3. In what sense does the law have dominion over a man?

4. How long does the law have this dominion (v. 1)?

5. What example does Paul use to illustrate his point (vv. 2–3)?

6. What do these verses teach us concerning divorce and remarriage?

7. How do these verses prove Paul's point (v. 4)?

8. What does "in the flesh" mean (v. 5)?

9. What are the "motions of sins" (v. 5)? What result did they have?

10. What is the great change described in verses 5–6?

11. Why does Paul speak in the first person in verses 7–25?

12. What does Paul mean when he asks if the law is sin (v. 7)?

13. Does verse 7 mean that sin exists only where there is law?

14. Why does Paul use the tenth commandment to make his point (v. 7)?

15. What is concupiscence (v. 8)? How is it wrought by sin?

16. What does it mean that we are alive without the law (v. 9)?

17. What is the coming of the commandment (v. 9)?

18. What does it mean that sin revived (v. 9)? How is death its consequence?

19. How is the commandment, intended for life, found to be unto death (v. 10)?

20. What does it mean that sin took advantage by the commandment (v. 11)?

21. How did sin deceive and slay (v. 11)?

22. What does it mean that the law and commandment are holy, just, and good (v. 12)?

23. What does it mean that sin might appear sin and that it might become exceedingly sinful (v. 13)?

24. Whom does Paul describe in verses 14–25: an unconverted person, an immature Christian, or himself and every believer?

25. What does it mean that the law is spiritual (v. 14)?

26. What does it mean that Paul is carnal (v. 14)?

27. What is it to be sold under sin (v. 14)? Is this true of the believer?

28. What conflict does Paul describe in verse 15?

29. What does it mean to consent to the law that it is good (v. 16)?

30. Is Paul avoiding responsibility by making an excuse in verse 17?

31. What is the meaning of "flesh" in verse 18?

32. What is Paul's problem according to verse 18?

33. How does Paul describe this problem in verses 19–21?

34. Is Paul again avoiding responsibility in verse 20?

35. What is the inward man of verse 22?

36. What is the law that wars against the law of his mind (v. 23)?

37. What is the law of his mind (v. 23)?

38. What is the law of sin (v. 23)?

39. What is the body of this death (v. 24)?

40. What is the answer (v. 25) to the question of verse 24?

41. What is the difference between serving the law of God with the mind and serving the law of sin with the flesh (v. 25)?

Romans 8

Romans 8:1–18

In this chapter Paul teaches assurance, another fruit of justification.

1. How does "therefore" connect 7:25 with 8:1?

2. What is assurance? How do we know that we have it?

3. What is "no condemnation" (v. 1)?

4. What does it mean that we are in Christ Jesus (v. 1)? How do we know that we are in him?

5. What is the law of the Spirit of life (v. 2)?

6. What is the law of sin and death (v. 2)?

7. What is the law mentioned in verse 3? What could it not do? Why not?

8. For what purpose did God send his Son (v. 3)?

9. What two kinds of people are described in verses 5–8?

10. How does this demonstrate the truth of the antithesis?

11. What are the things of the flesh (v. 5)? What is it to be carnally minded (v. 6)?

12. What are the things of the Spirit (v. 5)? What is it to be spiritually minded (v. 6)?

13. What does it mean that the carnal mind is not and cannot be subject to the law of God (v. 7)? Why not?

14. What is the contrast between the flesh and the Spirit (v. 9)?

15. What does it mean that if a man does not have the Spirit, he is none of his (v. 9)?

16. What does it mean that the body is dead because of sin (v. 10)?

17. What does it mean that the Spirit is life because of righteousness (v. 10)?

18. Although our sinfulness means that we die physically, what is true because of the Spirit (vv. 10–11)?

19. What in our lives proves that we have the Spirit (v. 11)?

20. What is the connection between our present regeneration and our future resurrection (v. 11)?

21. What does it mean that we are not debtors to the flesh (v. 12)?

22. Why is this true (v. 13)?

23. How do we know that we are the sons of God (v. 14)?

24. What is the Spirit of adoption in contrast to the spirit of bondage (v. 15)?

25. What does "Abba" mean (v. 15)? What is its significance in this passage?

26. How does the Spirit bear witness with our spirit (v. 16)? Of what does he bear witness?

27. What does it mean that we are heirs of God and joint-heirs with Christ (v. 17)?

28. What does Paul mean by "suffering with him" (v. 17) and "the suffering of this present time" (v. 18)?

29. What two things does Paul compare in verse 18?

30. What is the glory that will be revealed in us (v. 18)?

Romans 8:19–27

Paul speaks of three groanings.
First, the groaning of the creature (vv. 19–22).

1. What is the meaning of "creature" in this passage?

2. What is the earnest expectation of the creature (v. 19)?

3. Who are the sons of God? What is their manifestation (v. 19)?

4. What does its being made subject to vanity mean (v. 20)? How did this happen?

5. Who subjected the creature (v. 20)?

6. How does the biblical meaning of hope differ from our use of the term (v. 20)?

7. How and when will the creature be delivered (v. 21)?

8. From what and into what will the creature be changed (v. 21)?

9. What is the idea of "groaning" (v. 22)? Why does the creation groan?

10. Why is this groaning compared to childbirth (v. 22)?

11. How is the creature and its groaning connected with the sons of God and their manifestation?

Second, the groaning of believers (vv. 23–25)

12. Whom does Paul include in the "we" of these verses?

13. What are the firstfruits of the Spirit? Why are we described as having the firstfruits (v. 23)?

14. How is adoption defined in verse 23?

15. What aspect of hope is emphasized in verses 24 and 25?

16. What does it mean to be saved by hope (v. 24)? Does this conflict with being saved by faith?

17. Is hope subjective or objective?

18. How is hope related to patience (v. 25)?

Third, the groaning of the Spirit (vv. 26–27)

19. What are our infirmities (v. 26)? Why is it necessary that the Spirit helps them?

20. What is intercession (v. 26)?

21. How does the Spirit make intercession for us (v. 26)?

22. If Christ makes intercession for us (v. 34), why is the Spirit said to make intercession (v. 26)?

23. Why does the Spirit groan (v. 26)? Why cannot these groanings be uttered?

24. Who searches the hearts (v. 27)?

25. Whose hearts does he search (v. 27)?

26. How does he know the mind of the Spirit (v. 27)?

27. What is the will of God (v. 27)?

28. How is this will related to intercession (v. 27)?

29. How are verses 26–27 a source of comfort for us?

Romans 8:28–39

Paul describes the assurance that results from justification.

1. What do "all things" include (v. 28)?

2. How do we know that all things work together (v. 28)?

3. Why does Paul speak of those who love God rather than those whom God loves (v. 28)?

4. What is God's purpose (v. 28)? What does it mean to be called according to it?

5. Why is the last part of verse 28 added to describe further those who love God?

6. According to verses 29–30, what are the links in the commonly called "chain of salvation"?

7. What is the origin of our salvation (v. 29)? Why does this matter?

8. What does it mean to foreknow (v. 29)? What is it to predestinate?

9. Is predestination conditioned by foreknowledge (v. 29)?

10. What does it mean to be conformed to the image of God's Son (v. 29)?

11. What is God's purpose in predestination (v. 29)?

12. What is it to be conformed to the image of God's Son (v. 29)?

13. What does it mean that the Son is the firstborn among many brethren (v. 29)?

14. What is the idea of the calling (v. 30)? When does the calling take place?

15. What follows from the calling (v. 30)?

16. How does the order of calling and justification contradict justification by works?

17. What is the meaning of glorification (v. 30)?

18. How are verses 29–30 important for our assurance of salvation?

19. Why are the five questions of verses 31–35 important for our assurance?

20. What is Paul's first rhetorical question (v. 31)? What is the implied answer?

21. What is the second question (v. 32)? What ground does Paul imply in his answer?

22. What is the third question (v. 33)? What is the answer?

23. What is the fourth question (v. 34)? How is Christ's death, resurrection, sitting at God's right hand, and intercession the answer?

24. What is the fifth question (v. 35)? What possibilities does Paul mention (vv. 35–36)?

25. What is Paul's answer (vv. 37–39)?

26. What does it mean to be more than conquerors (v. 37)?

27. What can all of the elements mentioned in verses 38–39 not do? Why not?

Romans 9

Romans 9:1–13

Paul turns from justification and its fruits to the eternal cause of salvation according to the sovereign good pleasure of God.

1. Why does Paul use such strong language—essentially swearing an oath—in verse 1?

2. What is the conscience?

3. How does it bear witness in the Holy Spirit?

4. What is Paul's great sorrow (v. 2)?

5. How strongly does Paul feel this sorrow (v. 3)?

6. Concerning whom is Paul sorrowful (vv. 3–4)?

7. What eight-fold description does Paul use in verses 4–5? What does each of these mean?

8. Is the unbelief of Israel due to weakness or failure of God's word of the gospel (v. 6)?

9. What is instead the reason?

10. What contrast does Paul repeat three times in verses 6–8?

11. What is the difference between being Israel or *of* Israel (v. 6)?

12. What is the difference between seed and children (v. 7)? How does the example of Isaac illustrate this truth?

13. How are the children of the promise distinguished from the children of the flesh (v. 8)?

14. How does the example of Isaac's birth to Sarah demonstrate the word of promise (v. 9)?

15. How do Jacob and Esau demonstrate the truth of verses 6–8?

16. Why is the contrast between Jacob and Esau stronger than the contrast between Ishmael and Isaac?

17. What extra explanation is given for the difference between Jacob and Esau (v. 11)?

18. What is the purpose of God according to election (v. 11)?

19. What is the significance of "not of works, but of him that calleth" (v. 11)?

20. What does it mean that the elder will serve the younger (v. 12)?

21. What does it mean that God hated Esau and loved Jacob (v. 13)?

22. Are Jacob and Esau to be understood individually or as representatives of nations?

23. What Reformed truth is stated in verses 12–13?

24. Is the relation of election to reprobation one of "equal ultimacy?"

25. Is reprobation the cause of damnation?

26. What is the relation between election and reprobation?

Romans 9:14–33

Paul teaches that God is just in his double predestination, and he proves this from scripture.

1. What is the point of the first question in verse 14?

2. What potential objection against predestination does Paul raise in the second question (v. 14)?

3. How does Paul answer in verse 15?

4. Does this mean that God is arbitrary in his choices?

5. To what do willing and running refer (v. 16)?

6. Why are they not the cause of faith? What is the cause of faith (v. 16)?

7. How does the example of Pharaoh (v. 17) show God's righteousness and sovereignty in reprobation?

8. What does it mean that God raised up Pharaoh (v. 17)?

9. If the explanation for faith is God's mercy, what is the explanation for unbelief (v. 17)?

10. How does God harden the reprobate?

11. What is God's purpose in reprobation (v. 17)?

12. What conclusion does Paul draw in verse 18?

13. What objection is raised in verse 19?

14. What answer does Paul give in verse 20 in the first question?

15. What two questions does he use (vv. 20–21) to explain his answer?

16. Does God form a vessel unto dishonor against its will, i.e., are people who want to be saved reprobated against their will?

17. What are vessels of wrath (v. 22) and vessels of mercy (v. 23)?

18. What is God's purpose with the vessels of wrath (v. 22)?

19. What does it mean that God endures them with much long-suffering (v. 22)?

20. What is God's purpose with the vessels of mercy (v. 23)?

21. Who are included in the vessels of mercy (v. 24)?

22. When Paul quotes (vv. 25–26) from Hosea and from Isaiah (vv. 27–29), how can he use prophecy about Israel to refer to the Gentiles?

23. What does this tell us about the fulfillment of Old Testament prophecies concerning Israel?

24. How do these Old Testament quotations demonstrate the truth of sovereign, double predestination?

25. What is the idea of the remnant (v. 27) and the seed (v. 29)?

26. What is the meaning of shortening as applied to Israel (v. 28)?

27. What conclusion does Paul draw concerning the Gentiles (v. 30)?

28. What does it mean that although they did not follow after righteousness, they nevertheless attained to it (v. 30)?

29. How was this possible?

30. What conclusion does Paul draw concerning the Jews (v. 31)?

31. What is the law of righteousness (v. 31)?

32. Why did Israel not attain to righteousness (v. 32)?

33. What is a stumblingstone (v. 32)? Who is this stone or rock (v. 33)?

34. How does the stumblingstone distinguish between elect and reprobate?

35. Is salvation possible for the Jews? Why or why not (v. 33)?

Romans 10

Paul teaches that predestination is realized through the means of preaching and the call to faith.

1. When Paul speaks in verse 1 of his desire regarding Israel, does he refer to the remnant or to all Israel?

2. What is the zeal of God that Israel has (v. 2)?

3. In what way is Israel's zeal not according to knowledge (v. 2)?

4. What does it mean that they are ignorant of God's righteousness (v. 3)?

5. Is Israel's ignorance an excuse? What does it mean that they did not submit to God's righteousness (v. 3)?

6. What does it mean that Christ is the end of the law for righteousness (v. 4)?

7. What is the righteousness of faith in contrast to the righteousness of the law (vv. 5-6)?

8. What point does Paul make in verses 6-7 when he quotes from Deuteronomy 30:11-13?

9. What is the word of faith (v. 8)?

10. What is the connection between the word of faith and the preaching (v. 8)?

11. What is the relation between confessing and believing (v. 9)?

12. Are believing and confessing conditions to salvation?

13. What two promises are mentioned in verses 11-12?

14. What is their significance for the New Testament church?

15. What is it to call on the name of the Lord? What is the relation between calling and salvation (v. 13)?

16. What is the preaching, and what does it do (vv. 14–15)?

17. What is Paul's line of argumentation in verses 14–15?

18. In light of the correct translation ("whom they have not heard," not "of whom...") what truth does Paul state is the one who preaches (v. 14)?

19. Who must send (v. 15) the preacher? What implication does this have for our worship?

20. Why are preachers said to have beautiful feet (v. 15)?

21. What is the negative effect of the preaching (v. 16)?

22. What does it mean that faith comes by hearing (v. 17)?

23. What does it mean that hearing comes by the word of God (v. 17)? How is the word of God to be understood here?

24. According to Psalm 19, what are the sound and the words (v. 18) that are universal?

25. Who are those who are no people and a foolish nation (v. 19)?

26. How did Moses provoke Israel to jealousy (v. 19)?

27. Why did he want to make them jealous (v. 19)?

28. To whom does Isaiah refer when he speaks of those who sought not God and did not ask after him (v. 20)?

29. What does it mean that God stretches forth his hands to Israel (v. 21)?

30. Why would he do this to a disobedient and gainsaying people (v. 21)?

Romans 11

In this concluding chapter of the doctrinal section of Romans, Paul continues the thoughts of the previous chapters and essentially asks, "Has God rejected his people?"

1. In light of chapter 10, is it correct to conclude that God has rejected his people (v. 1)?

2. Why does Paul use himself as an example in his answer (v. 1)?

3. Why does he identify himself as being of the tribe of Benjamin (v. 1)?

4. Why does Paul use the example of Elijah to prove his point (vv. 2–4)?

5. What is the biblical idea of a remnant?

6. What is the meaning of the election of grace (v. 5) as applied to the remnant?

7. How does Paul define the relation between grace and works (v. 6)?

8. What process is described in verses 7–10?

9. For what does Israel seek but not obtain (v. 7)?

10. What proofs are given for the statement of verse 7?

11. Is hardening the work of God, the act of man, or both?

12. What does Paul say is *not* God's purpose regarding Israel (v. 11)?

13. What contrast does Paul draw in verse 12? What is "their fulness?"

14. What does it mean that Paul magnifies his office of apostle to the Gentiles (v. 13)?

15. For what purpose does Paul do this (v. 14)? What does "provoke to emulation" mean?

16. When Paul speaks of the fullness (v. 12) and the receiving (v. 15), does he refer to a national conversion of the Jews? Why or why not?

17. What does the example of verse 16a mean?

18. What figure does Paul use in verses 17–24? To whom is he speaking?

19. Who are the branches and the wild olive tree of which Paul speaks (vv. 17 and 24)?

20. Who are the root (v. 17), the good tree (v. 24) and the natural branches (v. 24)?

21. Against what error does Paul warn by this figure (v. 18)?

22. How does Paul admonish the Gentile Christians (vv. 21–22)?

23. What are the goodness and severity of God (v. 22)?

24. To whom is each shown?

25. What is it to continue in God's goodness (v. 22)? Does this make salvation conditional?

26. What is the only possible way of salvation for the Jews (v. 23)?

27. Why does Paul speak of a mystery (v. 25)?

28. What does it mean that blindness has happened to Israel (v. 25)? Why is it "in part?"

29. What is the fullness of the Gentiles (v. 25)?

30. Who is the "all Israel" that will be saved (v. 26)?

31. What proof does Paul give from the Old Testament (vv. 26–27)?

32. What does it mean that concerning the gospel the Jews are enemies (v. 28)?

33. What does it mean that touching election they are beloved for the fathers' sakes (v. 28)?

34. What does it mean that the gifts and calling of God are without repentance (v. 29)?

35. How have the Gentiles obtained mercy through the Jews' unbelief (v. 30)?

36. What does it mean that through the Gentiles' mercy the Jews may obtain mercy (v. 31)?

37. What do verses 33–35 tell us about God?

38. What are God's wisdom, knowledge, judgments, ways, and mind (vv. 33–34)?

39. Do these verses teach a hidden will of God versus a revealed will?

40. What is included in "all things" (v. 36)?

41. What is God's glory (v. 36)?

Romans 12

Paul begins the practical section of Romans, the application of the doctrines taught in chapters 1–11. In chapter 12 he begins with general admonitions, then speaks of relationships within the church, and then speaks of our relation to one another and to all men.

1. What is the connection between verse 1 and the preceding chapters?

2. What are the mercies of God (v. 1)?

3. What does it mean to present our bodies as a living sacrifice (v. 1)?

4. What are holy, acceptable, and reasonable service (v. 1)?

5. What is it to be conformed to the world (v. 2)?

6. What is it to be transformed (v. 2)? How is this accomplished?

7. What is the purpose of this admonition (v. 2)?

8. What calling does everyone in the church have both negatively and positively (v. 3)?

9. Of what truth concerning the church does Paul write in verse 4?

10. Of what truth concerning the church does he write in verse 5?

11. What is God's purpose in giving the church the gifts mentioned in verses 6–8?

12. What are the various gifts (vv. 6–8): Prophecy? Ministry? Teaching? Exhorting? Giving? Ruling? Showing mercy?

13. What does it mean that love must be without dissimulation (v. 9)?

14. What does Paul teach concerning our behavior in the church (v. 10)?

15. Why does Paul give so many admonitions in verses 11–18?

What do the following admonitions mean?

a. Not slothful in business (v. 11)

b. Fervent in spirit (v. 11)

c. Serving the Lord (v. 11)

d. Rejoicing in hope (v. 12)

e. Patient in tribulation (v. 12)

f. Continuing instant in prayer (v. 12)

g. Distributing to the necessity of saints (v. 13)

h. Given to hospitality (v. 13)

i. Bless those who persecute us and do not curse them (v. 14)

j. Rejoice with those who rejoice (v. 15)

k. Weep with those who weep (v. 15)

l. Be of the same mind one to another (v. 16)

m. Mind not high things but condescend to men of low estate (v. 16)

n. Be not wise in our own conceits (v. 16)

o. Recompense no man evil for evil (v. 17)

p. Provide things honest in the sight of all men (v. 17)

q. Live peaceably with all men (v. 18)

16. What if it is not possible to live peaceably with all men (v. 18)?

17. What does Paul teach concerning vengeance (v. 19)? Why is this admonition necessary?

18. What does it mean to give place to wrath (v. 19)?

19. Who is the enemy mentioned in verse 20?

20. How does caring for our enemy heap coals of fire on his head (v. 20)? What is the meaning of this expression?

21. How do we overcome evils committed against us (v. 21)?

Romans 13

After giving the principle of nonretaliation in Romans 12:19–21, Paul in this chapter applies it to our relation to the civil government, teaching how love for God and the neighbor must rule our conduct.

1. Why were the admonitions of this chapter necessary for the Roman Christians?

2. Who are the higher powers (v. 1)?

3. Why must we be subject to them (v. 1)?

4. How does verse 2 show the seriousness of disobedience to authority?

5. What is the two-fold responsibility of rulers (vv. 3–4)?

6. What is the two-fold responsibility of Christians toward rulers (vv. 3–4)?

7. What is the sword power (v. 4)? Does this teach anything regarding capital punishment?

8. For what two reasons must we be subject to rulers (v. 5)?

9. Why must we pay tribute (v. 6)?

10. What are tribute, custom, fear, and honor (v. 7)?

11. What does verse 8a say about financial debt?

12. How does loving one another fulfill the law (v. 8)?

13. How does love fulfill each of the commandments listed in verse 9?

14. Why is love the fulfilling of the law (v. 10)?

15. What does it mean that it is high time to awake out of sleep (v. 11)?

16. What reason does Paul give (v. 11)? What does it mean that our salvation is nearer than when we believed?

17. What is the meaning of the night (v. 12)? What are works of darkness?

18. What is the connection between armor and light (v. 12)?

19. What is it to walk honestly (v. 13)?

20. What are chambering and wantonness (v. 13)?

21. What is the difference between putting on Christ and not making provision for the flesh (v. 14)?

Romans 14–15

Romans 14:1–15:7

Paul addresses the matter of Christian liberty and specifically, proper behavior toward weaker brethren in the church.

1. Who are the strong mentioned in 15:1 and whose presence in the church is implied throughout chapter 14?

2. Why are they called strong in contrast to the other group in the church?

3. Who are the weak mentioned in 14:1, and whose presence in the church is implied throughout chapter 14?

4. What is to be the church's attitude toward the weak (14:1)? What are doubtful disputations?

5. Why does the description of weaker brethren center on food and drink (ch. 14)?

6. Why are they also described in terms of the observance of days (14:5–6)?

7. Why do some eat all things, but the weak eat only herbs (14:2)?

8. How are the weak and strong to get along with one another (14:3)?

9. What do servants and masters have to do with Christian liberty (14:4)?

10. To what does the esteeming or regarding of days to the Lord refer (14:5–6)?

11. What principle does Paul set forth in verses 7–8?

12. What reason or ground does Paul mention in verse 9?

13. What does judging the brother have to do with standing before Christ's judgment seat (vv. 10–12)?

14. What is Paul's conclusion in verse 13? What is a stumblingblock?

15. Does Paul teach in verse 14 that cleanness or uncleanness are purely subjective?

16. What is it to destroy a brother with meat (v. 15)?

17. What is the good (v. 16)? How and by whom can it be spoken evil of?

18. What does Paul teach about the relative importance of meat and drink vs. righteousness, peace, and joy (vv. 17–18)?

19. What conclusions does Paul draw (v. 19)? What does edify mean?

20. What is evil for the man who eats with offence (v. 20)?

21. What general rule does Paul spell out in verse 21?

22. What does Paul mean by instructing us to have faith to ourselves (v. 22)?

23. What does the last part of verse 22 mean?

24. What is the connection between doubting and being damned (v. 23)?

25. Why do those who are "strong" (ch. 15:1) receive the admonitions in chapter 14 and the first part of chapter 15, rather than the weak?

26. What is it to bear the infirmities of the weak (v. 1)?

27. How do we please the neighbor (v. 2)?

28. What example does Paul use to prove his point (v. 3)?

29. What is the patience and comfort of the scriptures (v. 4)? What is the purpose of the things that were written for our learning?

30. What do patience and consolation have to do with being like-minded (v. 5)?

31. What purpose does verse 6 express?

32. What is it to receive one another as Christ received us (v. 7)?

33. What principles in this chapter must govern our conscience and conduct especially toward the weaker in the church?

34. What principles in this section must govern our conduct toward both the weaker and the stronger in the church?

Romans 15:8–33

Paul writes about his motive for bringing the gospel to the Gentiles and of his desire to visit the church at Rome.

1. What does it mean that Christ was a minister of the circumcision (v. 8)?

2. Why does Paul distinguish between Israel (v. 8) and the Gentiles (v. 9a)?

3. What common theme unites the four proofs that Paul gives in verses 9–12?

4. What is the key idea of verse 13? What does it mean to abound in hope?

5. Who works this hope in us (v. 13)?

6. What is Paul's confidence regarding the church (v. 14)?

7. Of what has Paul boldly reminded the church at Rome (v. 15)? What gives him the right to be bold?

8. How does Paul describe his work in verse 16?

9. How does Paul glory in his ministry (vv. 17–19)?

10. Why were the Gentiles the beneficiaries of mighty signs and wonders (v. 19)?

11. How does Paul describe his previous missionary journeys (vv. 19b–21)?

12. Why did not Paul work or preach in certain areas (v. 20)?

13. What reason does he give (v. 21)?

14. What desire does Paul express in verses 22–24?

15. What are Paul's long-range travel plans (vv. 24, 28)?

16. Where does he intend to go soon (v. 25)? For what purpose?

17. Of whom does Paul speak in verse 27a?

18. What is the duty of the Gentiles and why (v. 27)?

19. Why does Paul describe prayer in terms of striving (v. 30)?

20. For what three things does Paul ask the church to pray regarding himself (vv. 31–32)?

21. What does he mean by his service (v. 31)?

22. With what blessing does Paul conclude this section (v. 33)?

Romans 16

Paul concludes his letter with many personal greetings and mentions many saints by name, and he ends with a doxology.

1. How is Phebe described in verses 1–2? What was Paul's purpose in sending her to Rome?

2. In what way did Priscilla and Aquila lay down their necks for Paul and for the Gentiles (vv. 4–5)?

3. Do we know where the church in their house was located (v. 5a)?

4. What does it mean that Epaenetus was the first fruits of Achaia (v. 5)?

5. What does it mean that Andronicus and Junia were kinsmen of Paul, fellow prisoners, of note among the apostles, and in Christ before Paul (v. 7)?

6. What do we know about all the people mentioned in verses 8–15?

7. Is verse 16a to be understood literally?

8. What sort of trouble does Paul describe in verse 17?

9. How does Paul describe the troublemakers (v. 18)?

10. How is the church to deal with these people (v. 17)?

11. What reputation did the Roman church have (v. 19)?

12. What does it mean to be wise unto what is good and simple concerning evil (v. 19)?

13. What promise does God give the faithful church (v. 20)?

14. What is the meaning of the grace of our Lord Jesus Christ (vv. 20, 24)?

15. Do we know anything about Tertius, Paul's amanuensis (v. 22)?

16. Do we know why Paul used Tertius rather than writing the epistle himself?

17. Who are the people mentioned in verses 21 and 23?

18. How is the mention of all the people named in this chapter part of the inspired scriptures?

19. What is the mystery that was kept secret since the world began (v. 25)?

20. What does it mean that now the mystery is revealed or made manifest (vv. 25–26)?

21. How do the scriptures of the prophets make this known to all nations (v. 26)?

22. Why are Paul's final words appropriate (v. 27)?

Notes

Notes

Notes

Notes